Funnier Bone Jokes

Happy Halloween

Kooky HALLOWEEN JOKES to Tickle Your FUNNY BONE

Linda Bozzo

Enslow Elementary
an imprint of

Enslow Publishers, Inc.
40 Industrial Road
Box 398
Berkeley Heights, NJ 07922
USA
http://www.enslow.com

Enslow Elementary, an imprint of Enslow Publishers, Inc.

Enslow Elementary® is a registered trademark of Enslow Publishers, Inc.

Library of Congress Cataloging-in-Publication Data
   Bozzo, Linda.
   Kooky Halloween jokes to tickle your funny bone / by Linda Bozzo.
      p. cm. — (Funnier bone jokes)
   Includes index.
   Summary: "Read jokes, limericks, tongue twisters, and knock-knock jokes about Halloween.
Also find out fun facts about the holiday"—Provided by publisher.
   ISBN 978-0-7660-4118-9
   1. Wit and humor, Juvenile. 2. Halloween—Juvenile humor. I. Title.
   PN6371.5.B68 2013
   818'.602—dc23
                              2012007713

Future editions
Paperback ISBN 978-1-4644-0176-3
ePUB ISBN 978-1-4645-1089-2
PDF ISBN 978-1-4646-1089-9

Printed in the United States of America

082012 Lake Book Manufacturing, Inc., Melrose Park, IL

10 9 8 7 6 5 4 3 2 1

To Our Readers: We have done our best to make sure all Internet Addresses in this book were active and appropriate when we went to press. However, the author and the publisher have no control over and assume no liability for the material available on those Internet sites or on other Web sites they may link to. Any comments or suggestions can be sent by e-mail to comments@enslow.com or to the address on the back cover.

Every effort has been made to locate all copyright holders of material used in this book. If any errors or omissions have occurred, corrections will be made in future editions of this book.

♻ Enslow Publishers, Inc., is committed to printing our books on recycled paper. The paper in every book contains 10% to 30% post-consumer waste (PCW). The cover board on the outside of each book contains 100% PCW. Our goal is to do our part to help young people and the environment too!

Illustration Credits: Clipart.com, p. 5 (right), 8 (top, middle), 10 (bottom), 12, 13 (middle, bottom), 14 (top), 15 (right), 17 (bottom), 21 (bottom), 22, 24, 26 (top), 29 (top), 32 (top), 34 (top), 35, 36 (top), 37 (right), 39, 40 (bottom), 43 (top); Photos.com: Anton Brand, p. 4 (right), Christos Georghiou, pp. 15 (left), 30 (top left), Cruz Puga, pp. 3 (middle), 33 (top), 38 (middle), Don Purcell, pp. 32 (bottom), 44 (bottom), Dynamic Graphics, pp. 6 (top), 9 (top), Ekaterina Gorelova, p. 5 (left), Elena Kostrova, p. 23 (bottom), grimgram, p. 4 (left), Julia Kelyukh, p. 40 (top), Kenn Wislander, p. 16 (top), laszlo lovasz, p. 33 (bottom left), Мария Пажина, p. 9 (bottom), Marija Bukarac, p. 41 (top), natasa radic, p. 11, ori-artiste, p. 8 (bottom), Petra R÷der, p. 30 (top right), Philip Roop, p. 6 (bottom), Rada Covalenco, p. 21 (top), Rebecca Lowe, p. 13 (top), seamartini, p. 41 (bottom), Simon Thornley, p. 26 (middle), Song Speckels, p. 15 (top), Stephanie Dunlap, p. 7 (bottom), Timothy Carillet, p 25 (bottom); Shutterstock.com, pp. 1, 3 (top, bottom), 4 (top), 5 (bottom), 7 (top), 10 (top), 16 (bottom), 17 (top), 18, 19, 20, 21 (middle), 25 (bottom), 26 (bottom), 27, 28, 29 (bottom), 30 (bottom), 31, 33 (bottom right), 34 (bottom), 37 (left), 38, 42, 43 (bottom), 44 (top).

Cover Illustration: Photos.com/Kenn Wislander (back cover); Shutterstock.com (front cover)

Contents

1 Tricks and Treats 4

2 Pumpkins 8

3 Skeletons............................ 12

4 Vampires 16

5 Bats 20

6 Ghosts................................. 24

7 Haunted Houses 28

8 Monsters.............................. 32

9 Mummies.............................. 36

10 Witches 40

Write Your Own Knock-
Knock Jokes...................... 45

Words to Know.................. 46

Read More 47

Index 48

① Tricks and Treats

What do you use to get wrinkles out of your superhero costume?

Iron Man.

Why did the little girl take a candy bar to her dentist appointment?

She wanted a chocolate filling.

Why did the boy put a candy bar under his pillow?

So he would have sweet dreams.

Limerick

There was a young man named Andy
Whose backpack came in very handy.
He looked all around,
Dumped his books on the ground,
And filled it with Halloween candy.

DID YOU KNOW?

Trick-or-treating takes place on Halloween when children dress in costumes and go from house to house. They knock on doors and say, "Trick or treat!" In return they receive treats like candy and other goodies. Did you know that it is thought this tradition was started because people believed they could stop tricks from being played on them if they gave children small treats?

What do you call people who eat your Halloween candy?

Parents.

The tricky thief took thirty treats.

What country did candy come from?

Sweeten.

Cheerful children choose clever creepy costumes.

TRICK OR TREAT!

What candy do kids eat on the playground?

Recess Pieces.

DID YOU KNOW?

Did you know that at one time trick-or-treating was stopped? It's true. During World War II children were not allowed to trick or treat because there was a sugar shortage. In 1942, people were asked to cut back on how much sugar they used. Many people sweetened their food with honey instead.

Knock, knock.

Who's there?

Isabel.

Isabel who?

Isabel working or should we knock again?

Knock, knock.

Who's there?

Shirley.

Shirley who?

Shirley you have some Halloween candy.

There once was a boy named Pete
Who liked to eat everything sweet.
He would go out,
Knock and then shout,
"Hey there, trick or treat!"

Knock, knock.

Who's there?

Scotta.

Scotta who?

Scotta be more treat-
or-treaters at the door.

Limerick
There was a young lady from Spain
Who forgot to get off the train.
She missed Halloween
In her costume of green
And never ate candy a-gain.

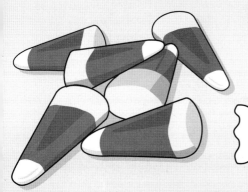

Carol carries candy corn.

If you have seven pumpkins in one hand and six in the other, what do you have?

Big hands.

Knock knock.

Who's there?

Maida.

Maida who?

Maida pumpkin pie.

What did one jack-o'-lantern say to the other?

"Cut it out."

FUN FACT

Pumpkins are a type of orange fruit in the squash family. They grow on vines and are harvested in October. They are just one of many popular decorations used for Halloween. Most pumpkins however, are used for eating. Pumpkin is used to make everything from soups to delicious breads and desserts. Pumpkin seeds can be roasted and enjoyed as a crunchy snack. Did you know that even the flowers from pumpkin plants can be eaten?

How do you fix a broken jack-o'-lantern?

With a pumpkin patch.

What do you call a fat jack-o'-lantern?

A plump-kin.

Peter plopped a pretty perfect piece of pumpkin pie on a plain paper plate.

What happened to the pumpkin who was always late for work?

He got canned.

Limerick

There was a young farmer named Drew
Whose awesome pumpkins grew and grew.
They grew out of hand,
Couldn't fit at the stand,
So he had to make pumpkin stew.

10

There was an old lady from Rye
Who was baked by mistake in a pie.
To the household's disgust,
She emerged from the crust,
And exclaimed with a yawn, "Where am I?"

DID YOU KNOW?

Did you know that carving jack-o'-lanterns began a few hundred years ago in Ireland? It's true! Original jack-o'-lanterns were carved out of turnips or potatoes. Irish families brought the idea to America, where they discovered plenty of pumpkins that were also easy to carve.

Plump pumpkins plucked from the pumpkin patch are perfect for a picnic.

FUN FACT

In early colonial times, pumpkins were used to make the crust of a pie, not the filling.

Skeletons

Why are graveyards so noisy?

Because of all the coffin.

Who snores more than sixty-four sleeping skeletons?

How do skeletons stay so calm?

They don't let anything get under their skin.

When does a skeleton laugh?

When something tickles its funny bone.

DID YOU KNOW?

Halloween would not be complete without a few skeletons hanging around. Besides being used as decorations, did you know that skeletons have a very important job that does not have to do with Halloween? Your skeleton protects everything inside your body and gives it shape. Make no bones about it, your bones are strong and light. Did you know your bones don't move? It's your muscles pulling on the bones that make your body move.

What did the skeleton order at the restaurant?

Spare ribs.

Who did the skeleton invite to his birthday party?

Anybody he could dig up.

What do you get if you cross a skeleton, a feather, and a joke book?

Rib ticklers.

Bring your big burlap bag of bare bones.

Joan's bones groan.

Knock, knock.

Who's there?

Fred.

Fred who?

Fred of dancing skeletons!

FUN FACT

There are 206 bones in the adult human body. More than half of them are in the hands and feet.

Knock, knock.

Who's there?

Sid.

Sid who?

Sid down and rest your bones.

What do you call a skeleton who won't get up in the morning?

Lazy bones.

HALLOWEEN DANCE

Why didn't the skeleton dance at the Halloween party?

He had no body to dance with.

Limerick

There was once a skeleton named Tony
Who was extremely skinny and bony.
When asked what he ate,
He showed me his plate
And said, "I'm just full of baloney."

I know a skeleton named Jake
Who constantly wiggles and shakes.
His knees cause a clatter,
His teeth even chatter,
But never a bone does he break.

DID YOU KNOW?

Did you know that Halloween is not the only holiday that uses skeletons for decoration? The Day of the Dead is a Mexican holiday that honors the spirits of the dead. On the Day of the Dead, Mexicans decorate their homes with skeletons. They also leave food and other gifts for the spirits. Like Halloween, many people dress up in skeleton costumes. The celebration takes place on November 1 and 2.

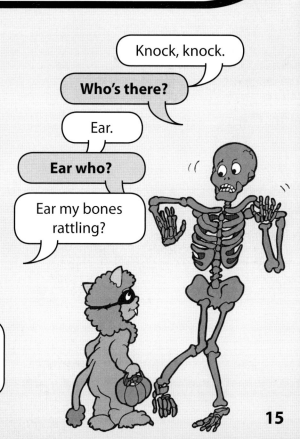

Knock, knock.

Who's there?

Ear.

Ear who?

Ear my bones rattling?

What do skeletons like to drink?

Milk, because it's good for their bones.

15

What kind of dog did Dracula have?

A bloodhound.

What's Dracula's favorite comic book?

Batman.

How do vampires stay healthy?

They take bite-amins.

What happened when two vampires raced?

They finished neck and neck.

Knock, knock.

Who's there?

Vampire.

Vampire who?

Vampire State Building.

DID YOU KNOW?

Did you know that the most popular vampire of all time is probably Count Dracula? He is a fictional character in the novel *Dracula*, written by Irish author Bram Stoker. The first *Dracula* book was published in 1897. The movie *Dracula* came out in 1931. It was the first talking horror film. It scared many people! Scary movies are still very popular around Halloween.

What kind of medicine does a vampire take for a cold?

Coffin medicine.

What do you call a vampire with a calculator on his head?

The Count.

Why doesn't Dracula have any friends?

Because he's a pain in the neck.

What did the vampire say after he had been to the dentist?

"Fangs very much."

DID YOU KNOW?

Did you know that vampires don't have to be human? It's true! Bunnicula is a character from a popular children's story. He's a vampire bunny. Now that's funny!

What do you call a vampire pig?

Pork-U-La.

Limerick
There was a vampire named Red,
Who slept with eggs and some bread.
And when he awoke,
He whipped up his yolk,
And enjoyed his breakfast in bed.

Good blood, bad blood. Blue blood.

Knock, knock.

Who's there?

Cheese.

Cheese who?

Cheese a vampire!

Vampires visit on vacation.

Limerick

A mischievous vampire named Little Bite
Gave his mother a terrible fright.
He went out all day,
Scaring kids away,
And now he's allowed out only at night.

Creepy characters clean coffins often.

5 Bats

Why did the vampire bat wake up screaming?

It was having bite-mares.

If the black bat bought a black cat, would the black cat bring the black bat back?

Limerick

There once was a bat named Matt.
Instead of hanging he sat.
He liked to chase mice,
Which made him think twice:
"Perhaps I'm really a cat."

DID YOU KNOW?

Halloween decorations often include scary bats. When people think of Halloween bats, they often think of the vampire bat. Did you

know that vampire bats really do feed on blood? It's true. They drink the blood from other animals. But they do not suck the blood. Instead, they cut the animal using their special teeth. Then they lick the blood up with their tongue. If a vampire bat does not eat for two days, it will die. Now that's scary!

What happened when the bat didn't brush his teeth?

He got bat breath.

Knock, knock!

Who's there?

Bat.

Bat who?

Bat news, let me in.

Why don't bats go out alone?

They would rather hang out with their friends.

How do bats line up in school?

In alpha-bat-ical order.

My pet bat Bertha likes to munch
A lot of insects for her lunch.
That's all she'll eat:
She says they're sweet,
And she likes the way that they crunch.

Where does a bat take a shower?

In the batroom.

What do you get if you cross a bat with a doorbell?

A ding-bat.

What does a bat wear when he gets out of the bathtub?

His bat robe.

How does a bat greet his friend?

With a sound wave.

22

DID YOU KNOW?

Did you know that bats are the only mammals that can truly fly? They can fly like birds even though they do not have feathers. There are many different kinds of bats. While some might eat insects, others might feed off the nectar of plants. But did you know that all bats have one thing in common? All bats sleep during the day and fly at night. It's true!

Knock, knock!

Who's there?

Bat.

Bat who?

Bat you'll never guess.

Black bat, brown bat.

The black cat batted at the black bat. Then the black bat batted the cat back.

6 Ghosts

Why is it hard for ghosts to tell lies?

Because you can see right through them.

DID YOU KNOW?

Did you know that hundreds of years ago people believed that ghosts or the spirits of the dead came out on Halloween night? That's right. People built large fires and dressed in scary costumes. Some dressed as witches and ghosts. Others dressed as skeletons. They believed the costumes scared the evil spirits away. But times have changed. Today, people dress in many different kinds of costumes. Some popular costumes are princesses, pirates, and superheroes.

What is the most important position on a ghost soccer team?

The ghoulie.

The greedy green ghost's glow grows.

Where do ghosts buy their food?

At the ghost-ery store.

Knock, knock.

Who's there?

Just ghost.

Just ghost who?

Just ghost to show you.

Where do ghosts mail their letters?

At the ghost office.

Boy ghost, girl ghost, no-guts ghost.

What is a ghost's favorite party game?

Hide-and-go-shriek.

FUN FACT

The Canterville Ghost and Legend of Sleepy Hollow are just two famous tales about ghosts. Another is The Friendly Ghost, about a ghost named Casper, published in 1939. Casper later appeared in comic books, cartoons, and even a movie.

Which room can ghosts not enter?

The living room.

Knock, knock.

Who's there?

Boo.

Boo who?

You don't have to cry about it.

There once was a ghost named Shrieks-a-lot Sue
Who scared folks away by hollering, "Boo!"
But when they booed back,
She went home to pack,
Then off to new haunts she hastily flew.

What did the ghost wear to the Halloween party?

A boo-tie.

What's a baby ghost's favorite game?

Peek-a-boo.

What do you get if you cross a ghost and a pair of glasses?

Spook-tacles.

Limerick

There was a ghost who liked to spread
Strawberry jelly on his bread.
He used to be white,
But oh what a sight
Since he turned a bright shade of red.

7 Haunted Houses

Why are there fences around haunted houses?

Because people are dying to get in.

What kind of insurance did the ghost buy for his haunted house?

Home Moaners Insurance.

How many Halloween houses has Henry haunted?

What color are haunted houses?

Boo!

Who wrote the new book about haunted houses?

A ghostwriter.

Limerick

A beautiful house in the woods I bought
Where ghosts would moan and lights flickered a lot.
From creaking floors
To slamming doors—
But budge from my home I simply would not!

28

DID YOU KNOW?

Did you know that people say the White House is haunted? It's true. There have been many ghost sightings reported there. The most common sighting is the ghost of Abraham Lincoln. Some people believe the Queen's Bedroom, where President Andrew Jackson slept when he was president, is the White House room that is haunted the most.

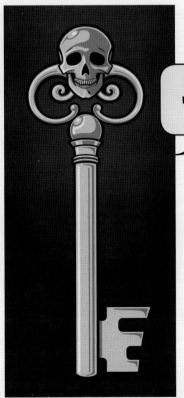

What do you use to unlock the door of a haunted house?

A skeleton key.

What happened after the monster ate the haunted house?

It gave him windowpanes.

Limerick

Strange noises and sounds you think you can hear,
But from where they come is not really clear.
The house on the hill?
It gives me a chill,
So I run away screaming, "Oh dear!"

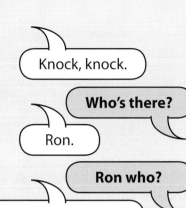

Knock, knock.

Who's there?

Ron.

Ron who?

Ron away, the house is haunted!

How haunted is Harry's happy haunted house on the hill?

Why are haunted houses so noisy in April?

That's when the ghosts do their spring screaming.

Why was the baby monster afraid to go to sleep?

There was a kid under his bed.

What kind of beans do monsters eat?

Human beans.

What do monsters drink when they're hot and thirsty?

Ghoul-aid.

Limerick

A monster at dinner is great
But don't serve his food on a plate.
You see, monsters will eat
Using only their feet,
And what a big mess they create.

DID YOU KNOW?

When people think of monsters, they often think of Frankenstein. Frankenstein is a fictional character from the play, novel, and movie of the same name, *Frankenstein*. But what most people don't know is that Frankenstein is not the name of the monster in the story. It's true! Dr. Frankenstein is the scientist who creates the monster. The monster in the story doesn't have a name.

What do you do with a blue monster?

Try to cheer him up.

What kind of monster likes to dance?

The boogie man.

Knock, knock.

Who's there?

Water.

Water who?

Water you doing for Halloween?

Limerick

There once was a monster named Dean
Who was never scary or mean.
When asked why not,
He gave it a thought,
And replied, "I like being green."

What do you get if you cross a monster and a chicken?

Strange eggs.

What do you get if a monster falls over in a parking lot?

Traffic jam.

What do you get if you cross a monster and a bowl of breakfast cereal?

Dreaded wheat.

What do you say to an angry monster?

"No need to bite my head off."

Mr. Monster's mittens are missing.

Where do monsters sleep?

Anywhere they want to.

Messy monsters make mustard messes.

Knock, knock.

Who's there?

Wheel.

Wheel who?

Wheel you go to the monster dance with me?

Limerick

A monster crept into my room last night
And woke me up with a terrible fright.
He said, "Who are you?"
I replied with "Boo!"
He was gone when I turned on the light.

9 Mummies

Why didn't the mummy go on vacation?

He was afraid to relax and unwind.

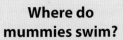

Why do mummies make excellent spies?

They're good at keeping things under wraps.

Where do mummies swim?

In the Dead Sea.

Limerick

There once was a mummy from Dover
Who asked if I could sleep over.
I went rather often,
Dragging my coffin,
I stayed with the mummy from Dover.

Why do mummies make good employees?

They get all wrapped up in their work.

DID YOU KNOW?

Dressing as a mummy for Halloween is a great choice if you want to scare people. But mummies in ancient Egyptian times were not meant to be scary. You see, the Egyptians believed if they preserved a dead person's body, it would keep the person's soul alive. That is why they wrapped the dead bodies in white linen. It was the Egyptians' way of keeping the souls of dead loved ones alive forever.

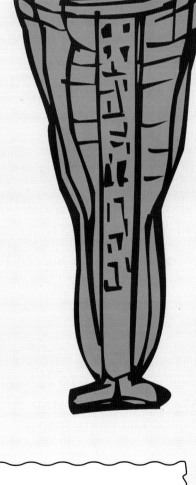

What's a mummy's favorite kind of music?

Wrap music.

How do mummies knock on doors?

They wrap as hard as they can.

Mummies make morbid music.

Knock, knock.

Who's there?

Ken.

Ken who?

Ken you wrap me up?

Limerick

**There once was a charming old mummy,
Who thought mice were awfully yummy.
He filled up his bowl
And swallowed them whole
Then later he felt pretty crummy.**

Why did the ghost cry?

He wanted his mummy.

What kind of juice do mummies like to drink?

Tomb-mato juice.

FUN FACT

Real mummies, with their coffins, are on display in museums all around the world. Did you know that there are not just mummies of humans? It's a fact. There are animal mummies on display as well. Check it out!

Many mummies meet Monday morning at the Monday morning mummy meeting.

Knock, knock.

Who's there?

Owl.

Owl who?

Owl get your mummy for you.

Funny mummies make more money.

Limerick

There once was a mummy who said,
"This wrap is killing my head."
But how can that be?
From what I can see,
That mummy is already dead.

10 Witches

What class do witches enjoy most at school?

Spelling.

Knock, knock.

Who's there?

Chuck.

Chuck who?

Chuck and see if the witch is home.

What do you call a witch who has poison ivy?

An itchy witchy.

Which witch is which?

What do witches' cats like to eat for breakfast?

Mice krispies.

DID YOU KNOW?

Many trick-or-treaters like to dress as witches. Witches and their black cats have long been a part of Halloween. They are known for casting spells and stirring their witch's brew. Wearing a black dress and pointed hat, witches are also often pictured riding through the sky on broomsticks—but not just ordinary broomsticks. Did you know that a witch's broom is known as a besom? That's right. A besom is a broom made of twigs tied together and attached to a long handle.

Why won't a witch wear a flat hat?

Because there's no point in it.

Knock, knock.

Who's there?

Butter.

Butter who?

Butter bring your broomstick!

Knock, knock.

Who's there?

Witch.

Witch who?

Witching you a happy Halloween!

Which way would the wicked witches walk?

What do you call a witch's garage?

Her broom closet.

Limerick

There was an old witch from Stewloo
Who made some potent witch's brew
From frogs and toads
She picked up on roads,
But she wouldn't eat it—would you?

What do witches put on their hair?

Scare spray.

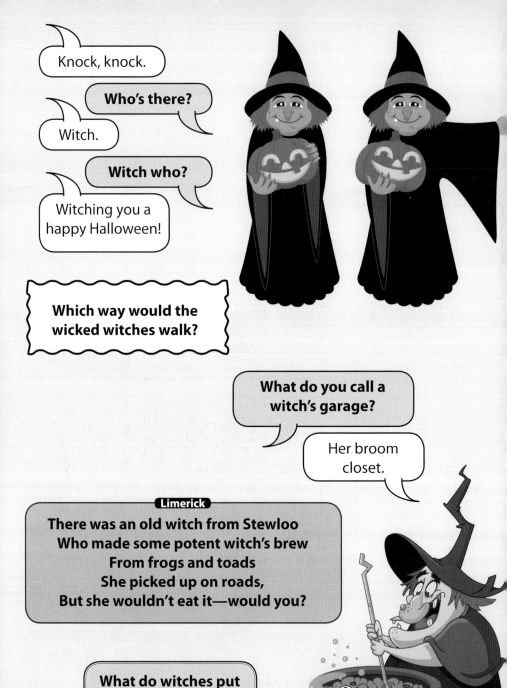

What do you call two witches who live together?

Broom-mates.

How does a witch know what time it is?

She looks at her witch watch.

Witches watch witch snitches.

What did the black cat ask the policeman?

Witch way did she go?

What goes *cackle, cackle, bonk*?

A witch laughing her head off.

FUN FACT

One of the most famous wicked witches of all time is the flying, skywriting, melting Wicked Witch of the West from the movie *The Wizard of Oz*. But not all witches are wicked. The beautiful Glinda, the Good Witch of the South, helps get Dorothy home by telling her about of the power of the ruby slippers.

Limerick

Wanda the witch, on her zippy new broom,
Came flying right into my living room.
She crashed into the wall,
But was not hurt at all,
Then she flew off again with a zoom.

Write Your Own Knock-Knock Jokes

Knock-knock jokes use a play on words to tell a funny story. You can write your own knock-knock jokes. It's simple. First, think of a theme for your joke. For example, you might choose to write a joke about monsters. Next, write the basic beginning for a knock-knock joke.

Knock, knock.

Who's there?

Then add a creative word or name like this:

Warrant.

Then ask:

Warrant who?

Finally, think of a punch line that ties in with your theme—in this case, monsters. You might write something like this:

Warrant you afraid of those monsters?

Now try writing a knock-knock joke of your own!

Words to Know

fictional — Something that's not real, like a made-up story.

harvest — To gather a crop such as pumpkins.

joke — Something that is written or said to make people laugh.

limerick — A funny poem that is usually five lines long, where lines 1, 2, and 5 rhyme, and lines 3 and 4 rhyme. Lines 3 and 4 are shorter than the other lines.

mammals — Warm-blooded animals that drink milk from their mothers.

nectar — A sweet liquid from flowers that birds and bats like to drink.

preserve — To keep from rotting.

riddle — A puzzling question that you guess the answer to.

tongue twister — Fun words that when put together can be hard to say.

tradition — A belief or custom handed down over the years.

Read More

Books

Dahl, Michael, Kathi Wagner, Aubrey Wagner, and Aileen Weintraub. *The Everything Kids' Giant Book of Jokes, Riddles & Brain Teasers*. Avon, MA: F + W Media, 2010.

Leno, Jay. *How to Be the Funniest Kid in the Whole World (or Just in Your Class)*. New York: Aladdin Paperbacks, Simon & Schuster Children's Publishing, 2007.

Phillips, Bob. *Super Incredible Knock-Knock Jokes for Kids*. Eugene, OR: Harvest House Publishers, 2007.

Internet Addresses

Giggle Poetry
<http://www.gigglepoetry.com/>

Jokes & Humor—Yahoo! Kids
<http://kids.yahoo.com/jokes>

Jokes By Kids—Halloween Jokes
<http://www.jokesbykids.com/halloween>

National Geographic Kids—Just Joking: Halloween Chuckles
<http://kids.nationalgeographic.com/kids/activities/justjoking/justjokinghalloweenchuckles/>

Index

A
America, 11

B
bat, 20, 22
Bunnicula, 18

C
The Canterville Ghost, 26
Count Dracula, 17

D
Day of the Dead, 15
Dracula, 17

E
Egyptians, 37

F
Frankenstein, 33
The Friendly Ghost, 26

G
ghost, 24

H
Halloween, 5, 12, 15, 17, 20, 24, 37, 41
Headless Horseman, 26

I
Ireland, 11

J
jack-o-lantern, 11
Jackson, Andrew, 29

L
Lincoln, Abraham, 29

M
Mexico, 15
mummies, 37, 39

N
November, 15

O
October, 9

P
pumpkin, 9

S
skeleton, 12, 15, 24

T
trick-or-treat, 5, 6

V
vampire bat, 20

W
White House, 29
witch, 41, 44
The Wizard of Oz, 44
World War II, 6